Alberto
GIACOMETTI

Why
I am
a sculptor

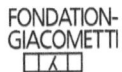
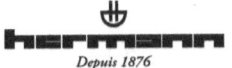

Notes sur la sculpture.

Je ne peux parler qu'indirectement de mes sculptures
et d'autant plus dire ce qui les a provoquées
Depuis des années je n'ai réalisé que les sculptures qui
se présentaient toutes finies dans mon esprit, je les recopiais
dans l'espace sans rien y changer, sans aucune modifi-
cation, sans me demander ce qu'elles pouvaient signifier.
(Il me suffit de devoir y changer une partie, chercher
une dimension pour que je sois complètement perdu
et tout l'objet s'abolit. Je ne vois jamais rien sous
forme de tableau, rarement de dessin et ça me
trouble beaucoup, les efforts conscients que j'ai faits quelques
fois pour réaliser un tableau ou toujours complètement
échoués.))

Mes sculptures finies je crois y voir, transformées et déplacées
des images, des faits, des émotions qui m'ont profondément
impressionné et des formes que je sens m'être très pro-
ches que je ne comprends pas. Je dois dire que les objets
que je ne peux le plus difficilement m'expliquer, qui
m'échappent ou m'étonnent me semblent les plus
vrais et les plus vivants.

Je veux décrire en tant qu'exemple la sculpture reproduite
ici et qui représente un palais

Cet objet s'est formé peu à peu l'été passé (1932) lentement
il devenait plus clair, les différentes parties prenaient leurs
places, leurs formes exactes et en automne tout avait pris une
telle réalité que dans une journée je pouvais le fabriquer
dans l'espace.
Cette sculpture se rapporte complètement à l'époque merveilleuse
qui prenait fin une année plus tôt, où pendant 6 mois
j'ai passé chaque heure à côté d'une femme qui concentrant
en elle même toute la vie posait chaque instant un plus
d'émerveillement pour moi. Nous construisions un fantastique
palais dans la nuit (les jours et les nuits avaient la même
couleur, la lumière du petit matin, je n'ai jamais vu le
soleil pendant cette époque) un palais très fragile avec des
allumettes, au moindre faux mouvement des parties s'écroulaient

finish the sculptures, make 2 new ones, exhibit them.
<u>write</u>,

Notebooks, 1933-1934

<u>I can only speak</u>
<u>*indirectly*</u>
<u>of my sculptures</u>

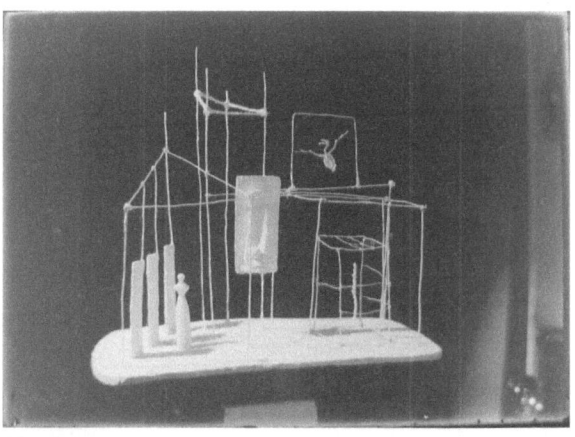

The Palace at 4 a.m., 1932
Photo Man Ray

I can only speak *indirectly* of my sculptures, and can only in part hope to express what motivated them.

For years I have only made the sculptures that presented themselves to my mind in a finished state, merely reproducing them in space without changing any aspect of them or wondering what they could mean (suffice it for me to begin to modify one of their parts, or to seek a certain dimension, to find myself completely at a loss and the whole object destroyed). Nothing ever appeared before me in the form of a picture, I seldom see in the form of a drawing. The attempts at conscious execution of a painting or even of a sculpture, to which I have occasionally surrendered, have always failed.

Once the object has been constructed, I have a tendency to rediscover in it — transformed and displaced — images, impressions, facts which have deeply moved me (often without my knowing it), forms which I feel are very close to me, although I am often unable to identify them, which makes them more disturbing to me.

I take the sculpture reproduced opposite for instance, which represents a palace. The object was created, piece by piece, at the end of summer 1932 and slowly became clear to me, its different parts acquiring their exact shapes and their precise place in the ensemble. By the autumn it had become so real that its execution in space required no more than one day's work.

It no doubt refers to the stage in my life that had concluded a year earlier, a period of six months spent hour after hour with a woman who, concentrating all life in herself, made every moment something marvellous for me.

We used to construct a fantastic palace in the night (days and nights were the same colour as if everything had happened just before dawn; throughout this time I never saw the sun), a very fragile palace of matchsticks: at the slightest false move a whole part of the minute construction would collapse: we would always begin it again. I don't know why it is filled with a spinal column in a cage — the spinal column which this woman sold me on one of the first nights I met her in the street — and by one of the skeleton birds she saw the very night preceding the morning on which our life together broke down — the skeleton birds fluttering way above the reservoir of clear green water in which the very delicate and very white skeletons of fishes were swimming, in the grand open-air hall amid the exclamations of astonishment at four o'clock in the morning. In the middle, the scaffolding of a tower which is perhaps unfinished, or perhaps the whole of its top has fallen in, been broken. The statue of a woman has occupied the other side, a woman in whom I discover my mother, as she appears in my earliest memories. I was troubled by her long black dress, which touched the ground: it seemed to be part of her body, and this frightened and confused me; all the rest was lost on me. That figure stands out three times against the same curtain, and onto that curtain

I opened my eyes for the first time. Captive of an infinite charm, I stared at that brown curtain under which a thin strip of light was filtered, all along the floor.

I can say nothing of the object on a small red board; I feel identified with it.

Minotaure, n° 3-4, 12 December 1933

Henri Laurens
by Alberto Giacometti

to Mrs Laurens

Once again today, on the first day of the year, I'm trying to write the text that's been occupying my mind almost exclusively for one week now, but each day the difficulty of finding words, of constructing sentences, of succeeding in composing a whole piece is becoming greater. Yesterday, I was sobbing inside with rage facing the total deficiency of my means of expression, facing those laconic, weightless sentences that don't express at all what I mean to say. However, I must try to do it well. The evening Skira asked me if I wanted to write this article, I didn't give a precise answer, but, almost immediately, I was taken over by a multitude of images that all referred to the region that is Laurens and his work. I no longer paid attention to what was being said at our table and for the whole evening, those images haunted me.

I could see, I could feel the bright street at eleven in the morning, "I'm going to Laurens", the yellow trees of the Villa Brune, the railway embankment. The high grey door of the studio. My anxiety at the moment of knocking "What if he's not at home?", my disappointment caused by the silence that persists, my joy on hearing steps approaching on the other side. Laurens' smile, the colour, the volume of his head at the moment the sculptures, in front of me, barely perceived, please my gaze.
Seen from behind, Laurens, one evening at dusk, walks

in the rue Saint-Benoît. The green leaves, a sentence said by him as he went by car to Mrs Laurens, in the countryside: "Here's our old house". The nice feeling generated by the relations of height and width when first seeing a work by Laurens. The immediate certainty: "This sculpture is very good once and for all."

Among those images, there is especially one that came back, imposed itself and gradually took the place of all the others, the only one that had no direct relation to reality.

I could see myself in a strange clearing, a vaguely circular space whose main colour was autumn leaves, whose quite close limits were lost in an atmosphere at the same time dense and light, and very soft. Around me sprang up, thirty centimetres above the ground and unevenly scattered, strange little hills that alternated with indefinable constructions, whitish, evoking small castles seen through a curtain of steam. But those hills, those constructions were complex, surrounded with resonances, and I could feel they were gestures, sounds of voices, movements, marks, sensations that had been, once, far from one another, in time, in the course of all those years.

Now those sensations became objects, simultaneously existed in the space around me and *filled me with delight*.

I first took them for my own memories, but yesterday, trying to write what I experienced in front of Laurens' sculpture, what I thought of it, I noticed, rather surprised, that with other words and by other ways, I was only reconstructing the small hills, the apparitions in the clearing. It was in that indirect way that this work had taken shape in my imagination, and that from the first evening when it was mentioned I should write this text.

Laurens' sculpture is for me, more than any other, a true projection of himself in space, a bit like a three-dimensional shadow. His way of breathing, touching, feeling, thinking becomes an object, becomes sculpture. That sculpture is complex; it is real like a glass (I'd like to say "or like a root", but I'm not so sure, though it is by certain angles, closer to the root than to the glass); at the same time, it is reminiscent of a human figure re-invented, it is above all else, the "double" of what makes Laurens identical to himself through time; but each of these sculptures is on top of that the crystallization of a particular moment in that time. (One could think it is valid for all sculpture, but I don't think so, in any case it's not in the same way, or at the same degree.)

The smallest part of that sculpture is worked and re-worked by the artist's sensitivity, becomes part of that sensitivity. Laurens only moves forward in his work with that absolute control and he never tries to disregard it. The dimension, the proportion, the movement of the sculpture are established, take shape and are finally determined according to that deep and complex sensitivity.

When working the clay Laurens also works the emptiness that surrounds the matter, so the space itself becomes volume. Laurens creates simultaneously volumes in space and volumes in clay. Those volumes alternate, balance, and together they become the sculpture. And that sculpture is a *bright sphere*. There are some black ball-sculptures that violently oppose the emptiness[1], black and white sculptures[2], sculptures that create a grey space of motionless silence[3], others, a compact space of darkness, as if they were hollowed in negative, in a dark mass[4].

I always experience Laurens' sculpture like a *bright sphere* that delights me. It's the same delight that I felt in the imaginary clearing.
This clearing, this circular space, was only that feeling of bright sphere became image and I found myself inside that very image.

Yesterday, while thinking about this text, I saw, with no apparent relation to what preoccupied me, the interior of the chancel of the cathedral of Bourges. I wondered "Why this cathedral, why this one and not another or a monument in another style, Renaissance, for example?" At the same time, I was inside the Santa Maria delle Grazie de Bramante, in Milan.
Then I understood the origin of that association. In those two places, inside the cathedral of Bourges and the Bramante's building, I experienced the same sensation of bright sphere. I remember having thought both times: "It is like an eggshell". We never really come close to Laurens' sculptures, there's always a

space of indefinable dimension that separates us from them, that space which surrounds the sculpture and which is already the sculpture itself. And I find again the dense and light atmosphere of the clearing and also the steam-like curtain surrounding the constructions in that clearing. It's the same sensation I often experienced facing living beings, facing human heads in particular, the feeling of space-atmosphere that immediately surrounds the beings, penetrates them, is already the being itself; the exact limits, the dimensions of that being become indefinable. An arm is vast like the Milky Way and that sentence has nothing mystical about it. Laurens' sculpture is one of the very rare that renders what I experience facing living reality and because of that, I find it resembling and that resemblance is for me a reason to love it.

I'd like to express myself in a more precise way on the qualities of that sculpture, but for that I would have to take up again the whole text and to give it another form, and I feel quite incapable of doing that today.

[1] Heads of Gudea.
[2] Egyptian sculptures from the 4th dynasty.
[3] Works by Pigalle, a sculptor who is no longer appreciated and whose name is reminiscent of a famous square, whose reputation is not without connection to that of the sculptor or rather, his oeuvre. For me, this oeuvre, more than any other, represents death; it does it in an implacable spirit that is not Christian or idealist (in the philosophical sense of the word). I think that this character, partly at least, costs the monument destined for Paris, its exile to Strasbourg.
[4] A certain pre-dynastic figure that is displayed in a window display at the Louvre.

Labyrinthe, n° 4, 15 January 1945, p. 3.

Monday night, exhausted, irritated, no longer seeing I had to stop completely but I don't really know in what condition I left my sculpture. I was no longer capable of any judgement but I was at the same time totally incapable of saying: it shouldn't be cast, it needs to wait for my return, and I let it go. Once again, as always, I think that work helped me a lot, that in the middle of the afternoon that sculpture was better than everything I have done until now; I also know what to expect from men walking (I could write 10 pages on that) but as for the actual result of this sculpture, I have my doubts, I think it is a catastrophe and I don't understand what pushes me to let it be cast and then perhaps I won't see the result and that annoys me. Should I let them send it to you in those conditions? I can't decide.

Letter to Pierre Matisse, 23 July 1949

The car demystified

The car is queen this week, since the Salon de l'Automobile has just opened and the Parisian avenues are transformed with gigantic gleaming car bodies. Well, everybody knows that the first model of a car, even before being sketched, is sculpted in clay. But what is the relationship between the art of sculpture and the beauty of a finished car? We put that question to one of the greatest sculptors of our time, asking him to share his reflections on the matter and to visit the Salon de l'Automobile for us. Here's Giacometti's article.

They are asking me what is the relationship between a car and a sculpture or even to what extent a "beautiful" bodywork could be a sculpture.

I went to the Salon de l'Automobile. Immediately, I was taken in by the social aspect: the competition, the presentation of the goods, money, class, struggles, pride, fashion and luxury. Besides, one is not really sure what one is looking at. One is impressed by the head of a visitor, the bearing of a female visitor. One sees rather ugly red, green, yellow blobs. One looks at flowers at the base of the cars. One finds oneself in front of a shiny black monster, huge, black and silver, that resembles a safe and conjures up a bank, villas on the Riviera, boastful men and loads of cash behind all that.

Such a car evokes the memory of crossing Paris in a similar car with such a person at a precise moment in one's past, with all the memories that memory awakens, another brings to mind a moment on a walk in the countryside, many many years ago. One looks at the dark ceiling of the huge hall and one thinks of the Gare de l'Est, the Eiffel Tower, 1900, Zola.

One rarely sees a car as a whole, one is attracted by a light, optical object, microscope, mechanical eye. Next, a bodywork drips like marmalade.

I look at a running motor, captivated by any machine as it functions, as the calculating machine that before the war had me stop, for a long time, in front of a shop window on boulevard Malesherbes each time I passed before it after visiting the Galeries, rue La Boétie, a machine that attracted me more than this motor.

During my visit, I didn't think about sculpture for one single moment. To be honest, once, there was something like a small *Victory of Samothrace* on the front of a car. Leaving the fair, by a strange coincidence (it was eight thirty in the evening) there was only one means of transport that we could use, a hackney carriage, no taxi. We took the hackney carriage. As we climbed down, I looked at the carriage, the horse, the cabman, that whole whose functioning was visible, clear and pretty, and which made one feel like drawing.

At times I've stopped in the street to look at a car. It resembled a toad, a bull, a grasshopper. In the same way as I stop to face a cloud that resembles a head, or a tree trunk that evokes a tiger.

The car, a new element like all machinery, is not only the descendant of the hackney carriage, but of the carriage and the horse together. A strange object with its own mechanical organism that functions with its eyes, mouth, heart, intestines, that eats and drinks, that functions until it breaks, a strange transposed imitation of living beings.

But the car, no more than the other machines, no more than all the pre-mechanical objects, has nothing to do with sculpture. All objects must be completed in order to function or serve. The more it is completed, the more perfect it is, the better it functions and the more beautiful it is. A more perfected object dethrones the one that was less.

No sculpture ever dethrones another sculpture. A sculpture is not an object, it is an interrogation, a question, a response. It cannot be finished or perfect. The question is not even raised. For Michelangelo, with the Rondanini Pietà, his last sculpture, everything starts all over again. And for a thousand years, Michelangelo could have carried on sculpting Pietàs without ever repeating himself, without going backwards, without ever completing anything, always going further. The same with Rodin.

A car, a broken machine becomes scrap iron. A Chaldean sculpture broken in four provides four sculptures, each part is worth the whole and the whole like each part always remains sharp and contemporary.

A broken Egyptian sculpture, a mottled Rembrandt, scratched, faded, blackened, still remain as beautiful a sculpture, as beautiful a painting as the day they were made. Contrary to objects that claim to be just what they are, a sculpture, a painting always claim to be something else than what they are. But there is – a new element, like the machines – abstract sculpture. It is concrete and not figurative. It can create and it creates finished objects like machines, only claiming to be what they are, and which want to be and are perfect. What are they, where are they situated?

A sculpture by Brancusi or another sculpture so-called abstract, rusty, dented, broken, a painting by Mondrian mottled, blackened, torn, what become of them? Do they belong to the same world as Chaldean sculptures, as Rodin, as Rembrandt, or to a world apart that would be situated close to the world of machines, the world of objects, and in what are they still sculptures, paintings, and in what are they perhaps not any longer?

Arts, n° 639, 9-15 October 1957

No sculpture ever dethrones another sculpture. A sculpture is not an object, it is an interrogation, a question, a response. It cannot be finished or perfect. The question is not even raised. For Michelangelo, with the Rondanini Pietà, his last sculpture, everything starts all over again. And for a thousand years, Michelangelo could have carried on sculpting Pietàs without repeating himself, without going backwards, without ever completing anything, always going further. The same with Rodin.

Arts, n°639, 9-15 October 1957

Farewell to Germaine Richier
Sitting among her sculptures

It is with sorrow and sadness that I've been informed of Germaine Richier's death. I think about Germaine Richier and her oeuvre throughout these past years. I think about all our meetings, the first going back in time to the period of Bourdelle and the Grande Chaumière.

I think about her enthusiasm, her passion, her tenacity in her work, my great joy at seeing her again, barely a few months ago, at her exhibition, among her sculptures. On the right, the powerful *Storm Man* and the very beautiful sculpture representing a woman, and, in front of us, the new works, new in every sense and that I have now clearly before my eyes.

My memory stops at that precise moment, sitting for the last time next to Germaine Richier, among sculptures that move me tonight more than ever.

Maloja, 2 August 1959.

Tribune de Lausanne, 9 August 1959

The Leg

You're asking me, I think, what led me to do the sculpture of *The Leg*. I've had that sculpture as a vision in front of my eyes since 1947, the moment I made *Arm and hand*. It was not possible for me at the time to make a big figure with various well-determined parts; however, I had the desire to define an arm, a leg, a stomach. I was only left with the possibility of making a part for the whole, and that actually corresponded with my vision of things.

I can't simultaneously see the eyes, the hands, the feet of a person who stands two or three metres in front of me, but the sole part I'm looking at carries with it the sensation of the existence of the whole.
That's one of the reasons I made *The Leg*.
But what counted at least as much, if not more, was the desire, the physical pleasure to have in front of me at a precise height, a foot of a precise dimension, the knee at such a height and the top of the thigh at that precise point above me, and what counted as much was the angle, the direction of the foot, the leg, the thigh with, in a way, the knee as a fixed point. On the other hand, the way the various parts were modelled counted for very little.

One day, in 1958, it became urgent for me to do away with that leg as quickly as possible after so many years of seeing it in my imagination without feeling a desire strong enough to realise it. That's all I can say today regarding that sculpture.

Paris, 13 February 1960

Why I am a sculptor
In conversation with André Parinaud

– Do you remember, Gicometti, the way in which you came to sculpture?

– It's so far back in time! It probably dates back to 1914, when I was thirteen years old. In 1914, I made my first bust from life. My brother posed for me. My father was a painter. I had seen a reproduction of small busts on a pedestal, and immediately felt like doing the same. My father bought me some plastiline, and I set to work. At first, I experienced a very strong pleasure, and I felt it was going to come very easily to me, that I would succeed in doing more or less what I was seeing – I still have the small bust at home. Fifty years on, I still haven't succeeded! It's strange to confess that in the last two days, I've been trying to make that head from the past, exactly like in 1914, more or less the same dimension as the first, and while in 1914 I felt I was doing what I wanted, now I no longer succeed. I worked till this morning, all night long. I had the feeling it was the first time I tried making a head. In fifteen days time, I'll see the next step.

– In 1914, you wanted to copy what you were seeing? To make in sculpture a photograph of your brother, for your work to be as life-like, as true as possible – the truth of the senses and the appearances? In 1962, what are you seeking to create with sculpture?

– To copy exactly as in 1914 – the appearance. Exactly the same concern.

– Where does the difficulty come from?

– Why, and that's from day one, do I feel like making heads? Why am I a painter? Why am I a sculptor? I have no idea.

– Do you continue to alternate painting and sculpture?

– Yes, every day I'd like to make a landscape, but I'm reduced to heads for the time being. Because if I "had" a head, I'd have all the rest; if one doesn't have the head, one doesn't have anything; that's the case for me anyway.

– But where does it come from, the facility you had in 1914 to make a sculpture you were happy with? And where from, the difficulty you're experiencing in 1962?

– It's very hard to say… Probably there was no difficulty between what I was seeing and the possibility to realise it. Today, it seems totally impossible. First of all, I no longer have the notion of volume, of space. In reality, it worked till 1920. My vision was evolving, but I could realise it.
Then, in 1920, I was in Rome, and I had a female friend pose for me for the whole winter, six months perhaps, and after, I threw the head in the bin as I was leaving. A total impossibility to seize the whole of the head.

– What was the psychological starting point of that reaction?

– Is it psychological? I don't know. But since, I haven't succeeded in making a head such as I simply see it, in the most basic sense. If I see a head from far away, I have the idea of a sphere. If I see it from close up, it ceases being a sphere to become an extreme complication in depth. One enters the being. Everything seems transparent, one sees through the skeleton. The main impossibility is to seize the whole and what one could call the details. Hence I only think of the eyes! One should be able to seize in a sculpture the head and the body and the earth on which it rests, at the same time one would have the space, and the possibility to put everything one wishes into it. Yes, one would need to sculpt the eyes in order to sculpt the whole.

– *Do you sculpt for the eyes?*

– For the eyes. Solely for the eyes.
I feel as if I could copy a little bit – approximately – an eye, I would have the whole head. There is no doubt, really. But it seems absolutely impossible. Why? I have no idea!

– *Could we say, Giacometti – without exaggerating – that your sculpture of a whole head has the purpose of carrying the gaze? Of trying to comprehend it and to pin it down?*

– I don't think directly about the gaze, but about the shape of the eye itself… about the appearance of the shape. If I could seize the shape of the eye, it would probably give us something that looks like the gaze!

Yes, perhaps the art consists in managing to situate the pupil… The gaze is made because of the surrounding eye. The eye always seems cold and distant.
It is the container that determines the eye. But the difficulty to really express that "detail" is the same as to convey, to comprehend the whole. If I look at you full-face, I forget the profile. If I look at your profile, I forget the full-face. Everything becomes disconnected. That's the case. I no longer even manage to seize the whole. Too many floors! Too many levels! The human being has become more complex. And in that respect, I no longer succeed in apprehending it. The mystery has been continuously deepening from day one…

— You belonged to Bourdelle's studio at the start of your career. What type of training did you receive from Bourdelle?

— It didn't provide me with much. We had to work with a life model and make a whole figure. I noticed that my vision changed every day. One day I could see a volume, one day I could see the figure like a blob, or I could see a detail, or I could see the whole. As the model was only posing for a very limited amount of time, he usually left before we could even begin to seize anything… Around 1925, I began to understand it was impossible to make a painting or a sculpture as I saw it, and that I had to abandon reality. From then on I created from memory — reality was forsaken — and that lasted ten years. I tried every possible way to construct until about 1935. As far as the abstract.

– What new thing did the abstract bring to your attempts?

– It was the last step before reaching "the wall"! The fabrication of volumes that were only objects. But the object is not a sculpture! There was no longer any possibility of progressing.

– You mean to say that your attempt to succeed in comprehending the world not by imitating it but by trying to seize it through imagination, intelligence, memory, by recreating it on the human elements of sensitivity, ended in failure, whose proof were your sculptures that were not living works but objects. But how did you grasp that?

– To make a living, I had accepted to make anonymous utilitarian objects for an interior designer of the time, Jean-Michel Frank. He was by far the best interior designer of the period and I liked him a lot.
So I accepted to make anonymous objects.
At the time, it was poorly regarded. It was considered a form of decline. I tried nevertheless to do my best as I made vases, for example, and I noticed I worked a vase exactly as I worked sculptures and that there was no difference between what I called a sculpture and what was an object, a vase! Of course, in my intentions, sculpture was something else than an object. It was therefore a failure. I had missed the point of the mystery, my work was not a creation, it was no different from the work of a cabinet-maker who makes a table! I had to go back to the sources and start all over again. Forgetting that in 1925 I had

abandoned the idea of working from life – because I found it impossible – I took a model again, wanting very quickly to make a study in order to make sculptures after. It was around 1935. Fifteen days later, I faced up again to the impossibility of 1925... and I kept the same model from 1935 till 1940. Every day, by starting every day, the HEAD.

– *It must have been terrible.*

– Yes. I sculpted exactly as if I was still at school. The more I looked at the model, the more the screen between their reality and myself thickened. One begins by seeing the person who poses, but gradually, all the possible sculptures intervene... between the person and you. The more the real vision disappears, the more the head becomes unfamiliar. One is no longer sure of its appearance, its dimension, nothing at all! In 1940, the heads became tiny, they tended towards their disappearance. I could only distinguish countless details. To see the whole, I had to have the model move back further and further. The more the model withdrew, the smaller the head became, which terrorized me. The danger of the disappearance of things...

– *From 1935 to 1940, you tried to conquer a face?*

– There were too many sculptures between my model and me. And when there were no longer any sculptures, there was a stranger so I no longer knew whom I was seeing and what I was seeing.

– How did the sculptures go back to life, suddenly?

– Why does one fall in love? I understood new phenomena or I grasped in a new way a very old phenomenon. How could I say? Have you noticed that the truer a work, the more style it has. Which is strange for style is not the truth of the appearance, however the heads I find the most similar to the heads of any person I meet in the street, are the least realistic heads, the Egyptian, Chinese, Ancient Greek, or Chaldean sculptures. For me, the greatest invention meets the greatest resemblance, it especially strikes me in the summer when I see naked women, they resemble Egyptian paintings, I mean by that the most symbolic art and the most recreated, the least direct... One could imagine that realism consists in copying... a glass such as it is on the table. In reality, one only ever copies the vision that remains of it at each moment, the image that becomes consciousness... You never copy the glass on the table; you copy the residue of a vision. I gradually understood the reality of a certain phenomenon one calls sculpture. When I look at the glass, its colour, its shape, its light, at each glance only a tiny little thing very hard to determine reaches me, that can be conveyed through a very small line, a little mark, each time I look at the glass, it seems to change, in other words, its reality becomes questionable, because its projection in my brain is questionable, or at least, partial. One sees it as if it disappeared... reappeared... disappeared... surfaced again... I mean to say it is definitively always between being and non-being. And that's what one wants to copy… The whole approach of modern artists is in that desire to comprehend, to possess something that is constantly fleeing. They want to possess the sense of reality they have more than reality itself. Anyway, one cannot possess everything… What one could possess is only the appearance. The only thing that remains of reality is appearance. If a person is at a distance of 2 metres – or 10 – I can no longer bring them back to the truth of a positive reality. If I am on the terrace of a café and only see people walking on the other side of the street, I see them tiny. Their natural size no longer exists!

– For an artist perhaps, but for a man the question is not even raised, it is what's normal.

– That I work or not, I only see superficially. There is no distinction. To such an extent that the landscape I see, the trees I see as I go from my place to the café, are every day a little different, which is new to me. Before the war, I had the impression that things were stable. Today, not at all. The world amazes me more and more each day. It becomes vaster or more marvellous, more elusive, more beautiful. I'm passionate about detail, the small detail, like the eye in a face, or the moss on a tree. But no more than about the whole, because how to make the difference between the detail and the whole? Details themselves make the whole… that gives beauty to a shape.

– What do you call "beautiful", Giacometti?

– Why does one find something beautiful? Why does one find a tree very beautiful? Or the sky? Or faces? And not banal? There are indeed people who find reality very banal and ordinary, and think works of art are more beautiful. For me, the question no longer arises! In the past, I used to go to the Louvre and the paintings or the sculptures gave me a sublime impression… I liked them in so far as they gave me more than what I could see of reality. I found them beautiful and a lot more beautiful than reality itself. Today, if I go to the Louvre, I can't resist looking at people looking at works of art. The sublime today for me is in the faces more than in the works of art… to the point in recent times when I have been to the Louvre, I've had to run away, literally run away. All those works seemed so pathetic – a rather pathetic way to proceed, so precarious, an approach stammering through the centuries, in all possible directions, but extremely basic, primary, naïve, to figure out a formidable immensity. I was looking with despair at the living human beings and I understood that no one would ever completely comprehend that life… That attempt was tragic and pathetic.

– *So why carry on sculpting?*

– I don't create to make beautiful paintings or sculptures. Art is only a way to see. Whatever I look at, it overwhelms me and amazes me, and I don't know exactly what I'm seeing. It's too complex. So one has to try copying simply to become a little bit aware of what one sees. It's as if reality was continually behind the curtains one rips away… There's still another reality… always another. But I have the feeling, or the illusion, that I'm making progress every day. That's what makes me act, as if I had to really succeed in grasping the core of life. And I carry on, knowing that the closer I approach the "thing", the further it moves. The distance between the model and me has a propensity to constantly increase; the closer I get, the further the thing moves away. It's a never-ending quest.

Each time I work, I am ready to undo without hesitating for one second, the work I did the day before because, every day, I have the feeling I'm seeing further. To be honest, I only work now for the sensation I have when I'm working. And if after I see better, if when I go out, I see reality slightly different, in the end, even if the painting has not much meaning, or is spoilt, I've gained something. I've gained a new sensation, a feeling I'd never had before.

– The work doesn't seem as important as the feeling you're experiencing?

– That feeling is without equivalence.

– Posterity – the idea of leaving signs – doesn't interest you?

– That leaves me completely indifferent. Signs, even the signs of the past, never become stable. They suddenly appear. They disappear. One thinks certain works of art have acquired a certain stability; it's not true. The *Laocoön*, which was a hundred years ago the masterpiece of masterpieces, is despised today. It has been put away, against a window, and no one looks at it. It's interesting to notice to what extent, at a time when everybody has to be interested in art, everybody likes or dislikes the same things. Any young woman who's working in the arts will tell you she likes the archaic, like everybody else. But she would be ashamed to admit she likes the *Laocoön*, which is as beautiful as the archaic works. Thus posterity is a lie, nothing ever stabilises.

– How do you explain that, for millennia, sculptors have wanted to imitate the world? And that this difficulty you experience when you create, they don't seem to have experienced it?

– First of all, till the eighteenth century, art was at the service of society or religion; the artist only conceived of his action as a necessity for the society he was part of. His work was a social secretion. Today, freedom is given back to him. On the other hand, the invention of photography and what it generated – cinema, television, X-rays, and the enlargement of reality with a microscope – has disrupted the view one has of reality. In the past, the only way one could have an idea of the outside world was painting or sculpture. There was no doubt about the wholeness of a head. For us, that bubble has burst. Photography gives a vision of the outside world sufficient enough for the artist to be free to paint his inner world, or his unconscious, or his sensations.

– So, in a way, you've been chased out of the world by the image and you have taken shelter, if I dare say, in yourself, in your sensations, in your lucidity.

– I distinctly began to want to work from life around 1945. There was for me a total separation between the photographic way of looking at the world and my own way of looking, which I accepted. It was the moment when reality amazed me as never before. Before, when I was coming out of the cinema, nothing happened, that is, the habit of the screen projected itself on the everyday vision of reality. Then suddenly, there was a rupture, what happened on the screen no longer resembled anything and I looked at the people in the cinema like I had never seen them before. And at that moment, I experienced again the necessity to paint, to make sculpture, since photography didn't give me in any way a fundamental vision of reality. Therefore, to know how I was seeing, I needed to try painting. Many artists experience a kind of terror of reality, because they imagine they will always remain beneath photography, in which they definitely believe, or worse, if they copy, their painting will be ordinary, or at best, it will be Impressionism, thus something that's already been done. So starting all over again is no longer worth it. For them, the world is empty!

– For you today, what is the adventure of painting and doing sculpture?

– To see, to comprehend the world, to feel it intensely and widen our capacity of exploration to the maximum,

but if one reduces a painting to three marks, the comprehension of the world is rather limited, all the more for, in almost all paintings – that struck me lately – be it abstract or tachist, fundamentally the vision is above all related to colours.
And the vision of colours has remained roughly the same as the one brought forth by the Impressionists. Therefore, one can say one hasn't advanced much in the vision of the world. For a time, Cubism was deceptive, but one notices today that the Cubists are now going back to a vision very close to the Impressionists. So it's still their vision that dominates.

– *Aren't the vision of the Impressionists and the vision of the Cubists fundamentally different?*

– Cubism ended with glued pieces of paper, erasing the work itself. It was enough to take a chair or an object and to present them for it to be a work of art but at the same time, it ceased creating works of art; the work of art has been obliterated. So what was needed was to go back to the sources. The word "going back" is already a defeat… And one hasn't really done much more than "going back".

– *Does this reflexion explain why you have broken with the Cubists and the Surrealists?*

– I was very attracted by Surrealism in its glorious days. It was the artists who interested me but in reality, during the time I belonged to the Surrealist group, I experienced things I thought were transitory. But

I imagined with terror that I would definitively be forced one day to sit facing a model on a stool. I felt that, in one way or another, I had to succeed.
And I did succeed. However, I know that art is only a means. Why that mania to want to be aware of what one sees? To what corresponds that need to try to paint or sculpt a head, it's nothing more than a mania!

– *Do you mean to say an artist is a being who's not normal?*

– Well, in a way, it's rather abnormal to spend one's time, instead of living, trying to copy a head, immobilizing the same person for five years on a chair every evening, to try to copy a head without succeeding, and to carry on doing it. It's not an activity one could qualify as exactly normal, is it? It even requires living in a certain society for it to be tolerated, for in others, it wouldn't even be tolerated. It's an activity that is useless for the whole of society. It's a purely individual satisfaction. Extremely egotistical and therefore shameful, basically! All artwork is born totally for nothing. All that time spent, all those geniuses, all that work, in the end, essentially, for nothing. If it's not for that immediate sensation in the present, that one experiences while trying to comprehend reality. And the adventure, the great adventure, is to see suddenly appear something unfamiliar every day, in the same face, that's greater than all the journeys around the world.

– This definition meets the adventure of the scientist who wants to discover the structure of the atom or mathematical principles.

– If one works hard at trying to seize in the best possible way what one sees, whether one works in science or art, the approach is the same. A scientist who specialises in any field, the more he knows, the more there's to know, and there mustn't be any hope either to ever reach a total knowledge. Besides, total knowledge would be death itself. Art and science are attempts at comprehending. Failure and success are completely secondary. This adventure is recent, it began around the eighteenth century, with Chardin, when one was more concerned with the vision of the artists than with the service to church or the pleasure of the kings. Man finally left to his own devices!

« Pourquoi je suis sculpteur », *Arts*, n° 873, 13 to 19 June 1962

The drama of a head reducer
In conversation with Pierre Dumayet

Giacometti's studio, near the rue d'Alésia, belongs to a time when painters used to make a vow of poverty. Outside, a woman in plaster, tall and slim, rusts next to the stairs. Inside, a narrow sofa, a table, a stool. One single bust is finished, for it's a bronze. On the floor, a few portraits and, all around, slender bodies in plaster, only roughly worked, waiting, back to the wall, to be executed, for Giacometti to look daggers at them, for he has a very critical look when he examines what he's creating [...]. He walks around in his studio. Look at Giacometti's face, born in 1901 in Stampa, a little village in the Italian Switzerland. His voice is as accentuated as his features. It's the voice of a tormented peasant who works the earth with his fingers. From his fingers the tallest – yet very thin – and the tiniest sculptures emerge. Giacometti holds one in the palm of his hand. It must be two centimetres long.

– And on top of that, *he says*, it's damaged, there's a leg missing, but one can see the belly and the breasts a bit.

It is a beautiful woman, in spite of that missing leg.

– On top of that – *Giacometti often says " On top of that", meaning it's the last straw* – not only is that woman tiny, but she's damaged, not only is she tiny, but she pretends to resemble someone: on top of that, for me, it's a portrait.

– *Who is it?*

– A friend, an English woman.

– *Why is she so small?*

– It's got nothing to do with me. It was in 1937. As it was still impossible to complete a head successfully, I wanted to make whole figures. I started them tall like that (*Giacometti shows the length of his forearm*); they became like that (*half his thumb*). It lasted throughout the entire war. Working every day, doing nothing else. I started them tall like that and when they were finished, irreducibly, they were tiny like that. It was diabolical.

– *Was it completely unintentional?*

– Completely.

– *And did you finally understand why they were reduced in size?*

– I understood later. The sculpture I wanted to make of that woman was well and truly the very precise vision I'd had of her at the moment I had seen her in the street, at a certain distance. So I was trying to give it the height that was hers when she was at that distance.

– *Today, do you still have the memory of that vision?*

– Yes; it happened on the boulevard Saint-Michel, at midnight. I could see the dark immensity above her, some houses; so, to realise the impression I had, I should have made a painting and not a sculpture. Or I should have made a huge pedestal for the whole scene to correspond to my vision.

– *Did you stop reducing your sculptures after you'd understood that?*

– Not at all. I understood that much later. No, to do away with that reduction, I decided one day to start a sculpture tall like this (*around one metre*) and not to surrender one millimetre under any circumstances.

– *Did you hold to that?*

– Yes, since I'd made that decision. But it became the opposite. Instead of being reduced like that (*in height*), it ended up being reduced like that (*in width*).

– *It was getting thinner and thinner?*

– Yes. I was appalled.

– *In other words, the extraordinary lengthening of your men and women comes from the fact that because of your discipline, you refused to let them be reduced? They narrowed because you refused to let them get smaller?*

– Well, yes.

– *You were saying a minute ago: "I understood much later", what did you understand exactly?*

– That one doesn't really see people life-size.

– Let's see. I'm standing one metre, one metre twenty from you, maybe. How do you see me?

– In the past, I would have seen you life-size. Now I see your head big like that (*around ten centimetres*).

– Not bigger?

– I see you exactly like that. What I mean is: if I make twenty drawings of you at that distance, I am sure in advance that they will all be the same, to the millimetre.

– And yet your head, at this moment, appears to me to have the size of a real head.

– That's because you mentally enlarge it. Because you know that my head has a certain objective dimension. And you imagine that dimension. But you don't see it. You see me small and you enlarge me.

Instinctively I close one eye and, with my pencil, I measure, from afar, Giacometti's head. It is around 10 centimetres high:

– The same size as mine, I said. Since when have you stopped "enlarging"?

– Since 1945. Until then, I had a photographic vision of the world. I thought photos were life-like. And then, suddenly, I saw the depth. The photo became a flat sign. It was as if I was seeing the world for the first time. Since then, I've been aware of seeing people as I really see them. It is marvellous.

Now, when I'm in a café, at the terrace, the people who walk on the other side of the street are tall like that (*like a thumb*). And the little woman who walks there, I can no longer bring her back to life-size. For me, and for you, if you accept to really see what you see, it's as if it was her size.

— *You no longer ever see people "life-size"?*

— No, no longer. Ever.

— *In other words, from the moment someone moves, he changes for you?*

— Yes. You here and you three metres from here, you are irreducible. You are no longer the same.

— *Perhaps it's the reason you've been making the portrait and the bust of your brother over and over again?*

— Yes; and I haven't really made it yet. From 1935 till 1940, he posed every morning. At that time, I was again making busts like I'd learned to make them at Art school: the model poses there, I make the bust. But I could only see details, and not the whole head. So, as I wanted to see the whole head, I made him step back. And as he was stepping back, the sculpture was diminishing, and diminishing…

– And when you find yourself facing a "life-size" sculpture?

– Actually, something terrible happened to me in the Louvre. In the past, I used to find the things I like in the Louvre more beautiful than reality itself. As if they were an exaltation of reality. Today, the people who look at the paintings astonish me more than the paintings.

– They astonish you?

– They terrify me. You see, the painting is a complete known. While the person who looks at it, now that I no longer see people "life-size", is totally foreign to me. It's frightening.
I like Sumerian sculptures a lot.
The last time I went to the Louvre, there was a woman leaning over the vitrine, and she was looking at a Sumerian head. That head immediately became a pebble roughly carved, and the woman became a marvellous object of which I no longer knew if it was material or not, a kind of transparent movement in space; a living object, the wonder of wonders. Now, I find everything that exists – this stool, the trees, everything – a thousand times more beautiful than works of art.

– Is it not disheartening to want to copy reality when one finds it so beautiful?

– I'll tell you a story. In 1956, a Japanese friend [Yanaihara] started to pose for me. He's a philosophy professor. He had eight days at my disposal before leaving for a three months journey across Egypt, Mesopotamia, and India. After having put his journey back eight days, he said: "Oh well, never mind Egypt, never mind India." And he stayed here, posing for me until his classes resumed. We worked all day. And in the evening, it was a painting. And the more it progressed, the more he disappeared. On the day of his departure, I said: "If I make another single line, the painting will completely erase itself." And I said to myself: "It's no longer worth it; if I want to copy as I see, it disappears." But then I asked myself: "But what is left for me to do in life?" To stop doing painting or sculpture seemed so sad that I no longer even felt like getting up in the morning or eating. So I started to work again.

– *With what hope?*

– It's no longer to realise the vision I have of things, but to understand why it fails. The idea of making a painting or a sculpture of the thing as I see it, no longer comes to my mind. It's to understand why it fails that I want now. (*Almost desperate.*) But I definitely see you, right? So why is it impossible for me to give that appearance? That's what I want to know. And the failing becomes the positive at the same time.

– How to explain that no one except you among the painters and the sculptors experiences that feeling of failing?

– Because today, one takes reality for a pretext.

– Is it the resemblance, the life-likeness that seems impossible to reach?

– The resemblance? I no longer recognize people through seeing them.

– You recognize your brother, surely?

– He has posed a thousand times for me; when he poses, I no longer recognize him. I want to have him pose to see what I see. When my wife poses for me, after three days she no longer looks like herself. I no longer recognize her at all.

– If you no longer recognize your brother or your wife, how could the portrait or the bust you make of them look like them?

– It's precisely that, I work to try to understand what is happening. For they end up looking like them for other people. When I do a head from memory, I'm told: "It's Diego." Personally I didn't know that. I don't notice details of heads, their characteristics. If you have to look at five Chinese people passing in front of you, in your eyes they are similar. But if you have to look at five White people, you distinguish them from one another immediately. For me when I see five White people, it's like for you when you see five Chinese people.

— *I suddenly think about what most people who love Giacometti's work like in you. They like what you consider a failure...*

— That's a joke! I am more or less the only one to make busts — of my wife, of my brother — from life. People who buy them are generally modern art lovers. They don't buy because it's a bust that's trying to be life-like; they buy because they think it's imagined, totally!

— *And you, what exasperates you is that it's not completely, really, exactly the bust of your brother or your wife.*

— Yes. At the same time, I think they are taken in. I think what interests them, even though they might not know it or wish to admit it, is that little degree of resemblance. But there's something else. If I managed one day to copy — it's what I'd like to know — to approach a little more the vision I have, what would it come to? A very conventional bust, possibly...

— *That would be the height of the joke.*

— That would no longer interest anybody.

— *Not even you.*

— Not even me (*correcting himself*). Well, that would

be the same to me. That would prove to me that, compared to those who were making those busts, I am no better.

– Do you sincerely believe that one day you'll be able to make – having succeeded in "copying" your vision of reality – a conventional bust?

– I don't think so; because of the fact that when I look at you, what I see doesn't resemble any other traditional bust…

Leaving Giacometti, I felt remorseful. Because of me, a man, who for forty years, has been searching for the same thing: to make a head, has lost precious time. The head that haunts him, at this precise time, is – for the moment – a dozen or so centimetres tall.

– Now, he said, I've decided not to give up on that head. I'll be patient. Even if I do nothing else in my life. And at the same time, it hurts: I would like to do trees, nudes. But it's no use for me to do nudes if I can't handle the head…

« Le drame d'un réducteur de tête »
Le Nouveau Candide, n° 110, 6-13 June 1963

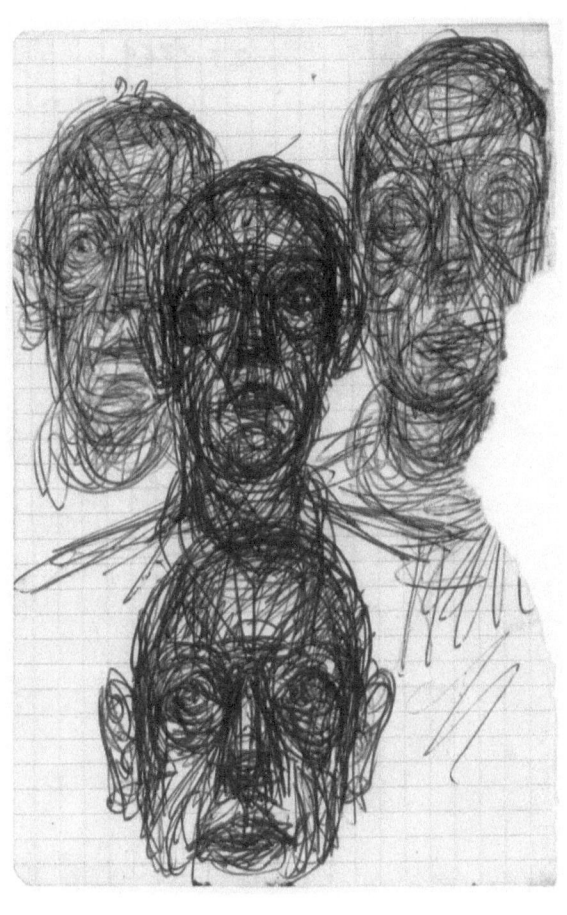

Four heads of men, c. 1960
Collection Fondation Giacometti

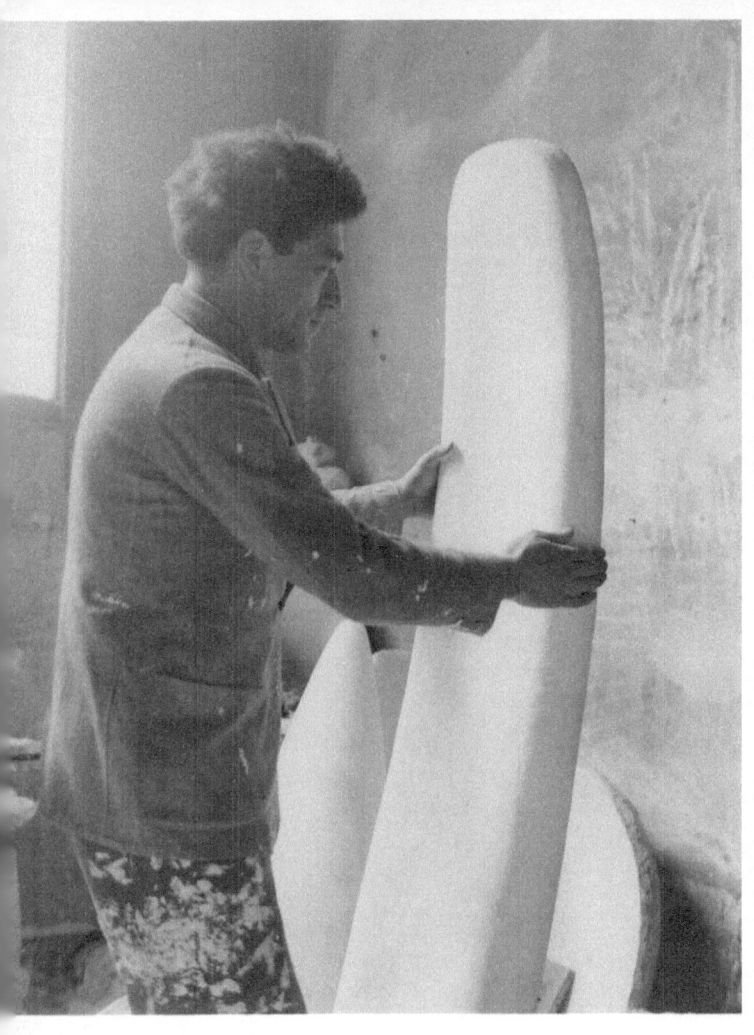

Alberto Giacometti in his studio, holding one part of Project for a Square, c. 1932
Photo anonymous

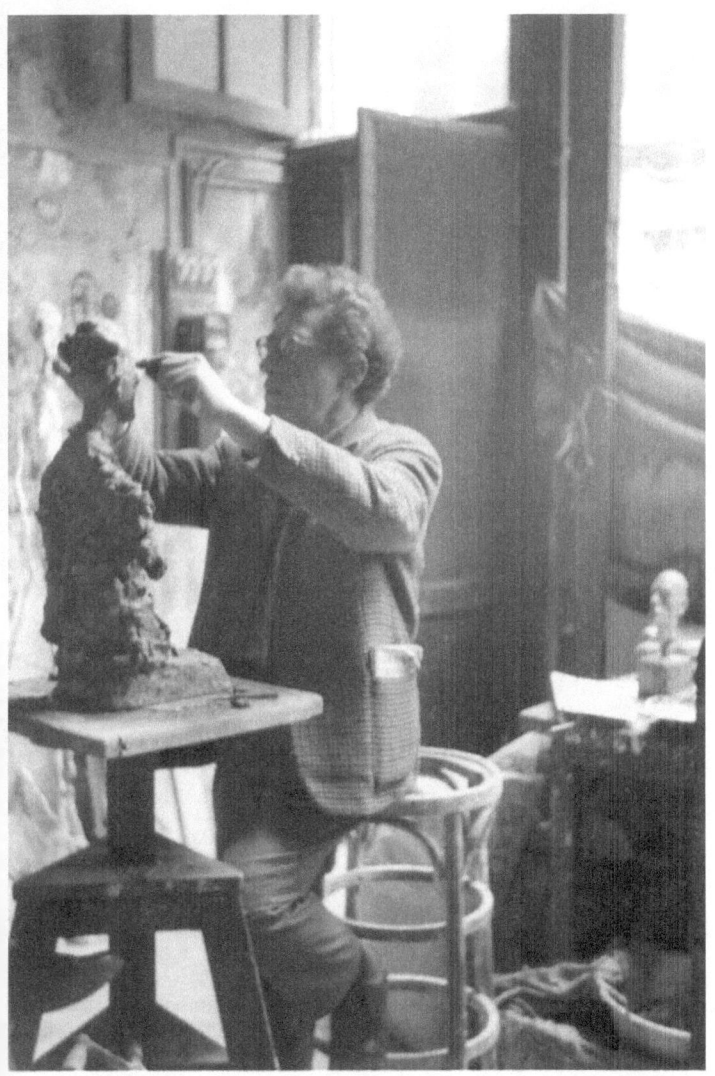

Alberto Giacometti modeling a bust of Yanaihara in his studio, september 1960
Photo Annette Giacometti

Sculpture, for me, is not a beautiful object but a way to try to understand a little bit better what I see, to try to understand a little bit better what attracts me and enthrals me with any head (…). If it's a little bit successful, a sculpture will simply be a way to say to others, to communicate to others what I see.

Les Lettres françaises, n°758, 29 January - 4 February 1959

6
I can only speak *indirectly* of my sculptures

10
A sculptor seen by a sculptor
Henri Laurens by Alberto Giacometti

18
The car demystified

24
Farewell to Germaine Richier
Sitting among her sculptures

26
The Leg

28
Why I am a sculptor
In conversation with André Parinaud

44
The drama of a head reducer
In conversation with Pierre Dumayet

Translated from French by Catherine Petit and Paul Buck;
texts p. 6 to 9 translation by Angel Gonzalez.

Cover: Photo Ernst Scheidegger
Collection Fondation Giacometti

ISBN : 978 2 7056 9407 4

© Succession Giacometti (Fondation Giacometti + ADAGP) Paris, 2016
For texts and artworks by Alberto Giacometti.
© Éditions Fondation Giacometti, Paris and Éditions Hermann, Paris, 2017
For the English edition.

www.ingramcontent.com/pod-product-compliance
Lightning Source LLC
Chambersburg PA
CBHW030503220526
45464CB00006B/2637